ABOUT *IMPOSSIBLE BLACKBIRD*

In Theodore Deppe's eighth book of poems, lyricism and a gift for narrative come together to explore the challenges and gifts of daily life on the coast of Connemara. Compassionate, humorous, utterly serious, these poems acknowledge the darkness of our times but also celebrate what they can. *Impossible Blackbird* opens with 'Lullaby Before Leaving' (shortlisted for Irish Poem of the Year in the 2023 Irish Book Awards), a poem of consolation during a time of change. Praised by Stephen Dunn for his 'Chekhovian eye and heart', Deppe introduces us to remarkable people at pivotal moments: an outsider artist and a twelve-year-old Bosnian refugee who meet in hospital; the singer Meat Loaf reclaiming his career in the wilds of Ireland; and Olivier Messiaen, who composed his *Quartet for the End of Time* in a prisoner-of-war camp. As Mark Doty wrote about Deppe, 'Witness has been raised to an art; everything is at stake in these painstaking, loving observations.'

I0867232

Impossible Blackbird

Theodore Deppe

Impossible Blackbird

ARLEN HOUSE

Impossible Blackbird

is published in 2024 by

ARLEN HOUSE
42 Grange Abbey Road
Baldoyle
Dublin 13
Ireland
Phone: 00 353 86 8360236
arlenhouse@gmail.com
www.arlenhouse.ie

978–1–85132–313–5, *paperback*

Distributed internationally by
SYRACUSE UNIVERSITY PRESS
621 Skytop Road, Suite 110
Syracuse
NY 13244–5290
USA
Phone: 315–443–5534
supress@syr.edu
syracuseuniversitypress.syr.edu

Typesetting by Arlen House

cover images:
three details from 'Winter in the Glen'
by Caitlin Deppe
is reproduced courtesy of the artist

Contents

For Annie

IMPOSSIBLE BLACKBIRD

LULLABY BEFORE LEAVING

'... to unpath'd waters, undream'd shores.'
– *A Winter's Tale,* Act 4, Scene 4

Frost warning, so into their beds
tuck the lettuce and spinach. Feel the cold
through the legs of our jeans.

We are leaving. We won't get to taste
this growth but it must be protected,
we planted it, we must give it a chance.

Where are we headed? Lettuce, spinach,
we don't know the least of it.
Even the weeds are luminous

under the Globe Theatre of the moon.
The stars are as unreadable as ever,
but I'd say they are auspicious. I'd say

for the moment we are all safe (no,
that's impossible) (yes, but just now it feels
that way, everyone has called,

everyone's accounted for).
Then the apparition of white cows, mud
over their spectral flanks,

a goodbye party from up the hill
that makes us laugh. Startled
when they see us, they continue

down the peninsula. Where
are we headed? To the unpathed,
to the undreamed, to the benedictions

of water and shore. Come inside
and sleep before the journey. The garden –
we must leave it behind – is all tucked in.

One Moment

One moment I'm walking home under stars so bright
    no flashlight is needed,

next I'm ducking into a neighbour's banger
    as hail pounds down

and whitens the night and I'm grateful
    islanders don't lock their cars.

Fatherly smell of pipe tobacco in the snug, dark VW.
    A staccato clatter surrounds me.

And just like that it's over and I'm walking again
    beneath brilliant stars,

Cape Clear spread out beneath me as I ponder
    the just-like-that-ness of the world.

One moment I'm dining with my parents
    in Galway's Pasta Paradiso,

revelling in the spicy main course, Road to Hell.
    Next moment

both parents are gone. Even the restaurant. Gone.
    Like a constellation

linked by imagined lines, I join moment
    to moment, making a story

that becomes this life in which I walk fast,
    leave doors unlocked,

strive to stay grateful, and keep glancing at the cloud
    that's already blurring the western sky.

Cordelia

for Annie

An island pub with a concert room upstairs,
which tonight becomes a theatre
where twelve actors from Galway

perform *Lear,*
backed by a storm at the windows.
At the afterparty

the poor doomed king chats up Goneril. The fool
laughs with Gloucester
who keeps rubbing his eyes. Cordelia –

sitting by herself, nursing
a hot whiskey, maybe fighting a cold –
is joined by an islander

who claims to own the oldest goose
in Ireland.
A Kerryman held that honour

until last week.
The islander asks if Cordelia can live
on her acting,

and she confides she quit her day job
to give herself
a year to write plays. Asked if she's sold

anything yet, she says, *Sure,*
my television, and the piano I never
quite learned to play.

What does she write about, the islander
inquires, and she ventures
Things that are just under the surface.

The mysteries
that hold us together. The Earl of Kent,
standing now beside them,

asks how one holds
anything
together, and she excuses herself,

finds a window seat
in the next room where she can scribble down
a few words:

there is a narrative she hopes will come later,
but the music at its core
circles back to childhood and makes her

want to weep:
something to do with harbour lights
in horizontal rain;

something to do with enough shelter
to make up stories;
something to do with the calmness

in the mad king's voice:
When thou dost ask me blessing, I'll kneel down
and ask of thee forgiveness.

The Quarrel

Seen from the dinner table, the double rainbow
puts an end to talk about Vladimir Putin,
and prompts our guests to stories about fog bows,
sun dogs, snow bows and moon bows,
but when Annie and I describe
the rainbow that, years ago, raced across Roaringwater Bay
and turned the path we were walking on

radiant, everyone thinks we're telling a story.
Siobhán types into her phone, 'Can you really
stand inside a rainbow?' and some expert assures her
it's impossible. Which means Annie and I
once stepped into a miracle. For one moment
we were bathed in fragments of light, and then it was over.
Like all miracles, almost too brief to be believed.

We'd been touched by the inexplicable,
and though we'd squabbled that morning
about whether to buy a house on Cape Clear Island,
three thousand miles from what we thought was home,
there was wild proof that at least for that minute
we were in exactly the right place.
Hard to argue about being luminous.

Tumult at the Harbour's Mouth

A fever of gannets, diving in fish frenzy.
Like the dream I had the night

Annie returned home from emergency appendectomy:

I sailed to Fastnet lighthouse
in a boat with seven women –

Think Virginia Woolf, I said in the dream,

Think Freud, said Annie.
But then I was underwater, watching

gannets drill through the waves,

inches from each other but not colliding.
On the same day surgery saved Annie,

our Cape Clear friend Paddy

died from motor neurone disease.
Earlier that year, he'd stationed

his wheelchair at the window

where he could watch the harbour mouth.
Look for whales when the gannets are diving

he told his young daughter, Treasa. *Life*

concentrates around life.
Towards the end, after his muscles

were so far gone he couldn't move anything

but his eyes and mouth,
Treasa translated for friends who came to visit

though words were almost unnecessary.

She nestled in his lap. Took her father's arms
and wrapped herself inside them.

Souvenir from the Gone World

for Kate and Joan Newmann

The blue letters on the worn canvas
of the carpenter's apron
read

Deppe Lumber Company
Phone 223
Baraboo, Wis.

Two pockets: one for nails
and one for star charts
or whatever one needs

at the top of a ladder
in that mythic place: Baraboo
of the river ferry,

Baraboo of the Ringling Brothers,
Baraboo of swirling Devil's Lake.
Years ago,

before travelling to my father's birthplace,
I asked the address
of his childhood home

and was told, *It's on Second Avenue –*
You go down a little hill,
then halfway up a hill – ask

at Deppe Lumber, they'll know
the house number.
This was after Mother's death

and Dad was 90, he was living
in a smaller place,
he was giving things away,

slowly divesting himself
of house numbers
and phone numbers.

He said, *You need to forget*
unimportant things
so you can hold on to what lasts.

Turns out Deppe Lumber had closed
a decade ago.
Still, Dad would have been able

to find the homeplace:
going *down a little hill*
then halfway up a hill

proved just right: we matched
the snapshot he gave us
to the house.

Two pockets:
one for forgetting,
one for memories.

My father remembered
sitting on those front steps
in the evening, his father

newly-dead, and hearing the trumpeting
of chained elephants
from the circus grounds.

They let us give them water
when they came to town.
They were a few blocks away

but when they cried out,
it felt like all Baraboo
was weeping.

Mr Imagination's Visit to Natchaug Hospital

27 February 1994

The poor. The broken. The blazing girl
who has not yet been diagnosed bipolar.
The ponytailed boy who sings in Greek

and has just been told he's schizophrenic.
The preacher's anorexic daughter, pale crescent
of a waning moon. The gang member

who has panic attacks and is doing time
in our adolescent unit instead of jail.
All of them trusted him, loved him, saw that he too

had journeyed rough. From flattened bottle caps,
his glittering vest, his majestic headdress,
his sceptre. And if this self-taught Chicago artist

carried himself like royalty, he spoke in a voice
that was gentle, urgent, and often funny,
even as he told his story. Shot twice

and left for dead. Then waking
from a six-week coma with memories
of past lives: an Ethiopian prince; a king

of somewhere; an Egyptian pharaoh.
He urged us to use our imagination to connect
with what is most real in us. Which is not

a contradiction. Make up something
that reflects our deepest selves. His gifts
of small blocks of industrial sandstone.

Most people might see those pale chunks
as waste from making steel, but nothing
is worthless, anything can become art.

When I look into a block of sandstone, I see images
of black kings and queens and have to start carving.
Carpenter's nails for each of us. But since

our twelve-year-old refugee from Bosnia
was on suicide watch and couldn't have
anything sharp, he made her a present,

carving her name into sandstone
then placing a crown above the letters: ^^^
ROZA
Listen. You must get in touch with whatever is divine

in you. Remember who you are and where
you came from. Where Roza came from:
a flattened village thirty miles from Sarajevo.

Sewn back together countless times,
a toy giraffe. The one thing her younger sister,
now dead, managed to grab from their burning house.

All these years later, an internet search told me nothing
about what happened to Roza. At least, no obituary.
Though I did learn that Mr Imagination is dead.

A photo of him sitting in glistening bottle-cap splendor
on the throne he fashioned from an old chair. Surely
the same throne he described during his visit,

though he joked that it was usually his beloved dog
who claimed that royal seat, grinning at him, reigning
supreme. Also, the image of a sarcophagus

he carved from sandstone with himself
stretched out inside, dressed like a pharaoh.
A sculpture that recalls his time in coma.

At his feet, the nail he used to carve
that grave which was not a grave but a boat
in which he lay on his back, journeying through light.

Sometimes, he said, *fear has seized me.*
And after fire destroyed my home and most of my art
I felt so down I could barely eat.

But forget fear. Forget despair. Just try to carve
an image of your true face. All it takes
is to see yourself as radiant. All it takes is a nail.

Mr Imagination Considers Chronology

When fire destroyed his home
and studio, Mr Imagination
found a wood slab on which to mount

a blackened, partly-melted
plastic clock
and named his sculpture *Time.*

He brought it to his next home
and found a place for it
in the new shrine he began.

I would always turn
every place I ever lived
into a shrine.

An almost timeless place, with no other
clocks. No calendars. Everything either
before or after the day of the robbery

when he was shot. And not just
the visions he had of past lives
when he was comatose. He said

he'd looked into a mirror before
the attack and caught
his reflection. Regally attired, like a pharaoh.

Even as a child he'd walked
a trash-lined backstreet
and seen a ball of otherworldly light

rise out of the blacktop.
No one had to teach him: Art, he said,
was his practice for recycling the past.

Of salvaging what is sacred.
Of making something transcendent
to greet what comes next.

For a time, the objects he preferred
were like that timepiece. Smoke-damaged
or charred from the terrible fire.

Everything had its afterlife.
Even an alarm clock
could be refined. Purified. Blasted.

Still Listening for the Coyle Brothers

When my wife asked, I didn't think I needed
anything for Christmas, but this afternoon

in an antique shop I've found a milk bottle.
Printed in red on the glass: *Paradise Farms*. If it hints

at a time of innocence, it also recalls
the 1959 killing of a patrolman who tried to stop

two bandits stealing milk from a front porch.
Soon, I'm also longing for the vintage wanted posters

I've found online for the Coyle brothers.
When I was eight, a roadblock delayed

our family's holiday, and an armed policeman
told my father to leave the car keys in the ignition

so the killers wouldn't enter our house.
Now, I want a Christmas call from my sister.

What does she remember of the train ride
the family took at Edaville Railroad

through cranberry bogs and woods, trying
to enjoy ourselves during a manhunt?

The sound-chord of the engine's whistle
rhymed terror and delight. And that night,

hearing noises in the kitchen, my sister and I
woke our parents, which meant our father,

to our horror, must confront the killers. Armed
with a slipper, he descended the stairs

only to find a litter of mice rattling the silverware.
It is almost Christmas, maybe I also want

the galvanized milk box, with its drawing
of a narrow lane winding towards a barn

that was Paradise. Decades after
the Coyle brothers, I flew four thousand miles

to be at my father's side. Not, it turned out,
for life-changing conversations, but to watch

television together. Wimbledon. Everything important
between volleys, present but unspoken.

That final night, my brother kept watch at the hospital
and I slept in my father's house, in my father's bed,

my head on my father's pillow. Then tried to decipher
strange noises coming from the kitchen.

And remembered Father walking downstairs, armed
with nothing, really. Armed, as we all are, with nothing.

On Three Poems by Galway Kinnell

Armed with a shoe, I investigate
night noise in the kitchen, but the intruder is
Galway Kinnell, helping himself to leftover pizza.
Turning, he offers a slice of my own pie.
Yesterday's feast always attracts ghosts.

That morning, making breakfast, I argue
with my dream's logic: it's not pizza
we should have shared, but oatmeal,
as in his poem of that name. During the kingdom
of time when stirabout is stirred, I try to make sense

of Kinnell being gone, he, who once seemed
the poet of *is*, whose fourteen-word poem 'Prayer'
pulled off the syntactical miracle
of repeating the word *is*
like lines of breaking waves:

> 'Whatever happens, whatever
> *what is* is is what
> I want. Only that. But that.'

I've always thought the poem was about *being*,
about *existence*, about *is*, but now I see how the word

what is used four times, so I pinch
sea salt into porridge, pondering what 'whatness' is
as constellations rise from the centre of things.
What I would have liked to tell him, if my dream
had continued, was that forty years ago,

working nights on a four-bed ICU in Kentucky,
I read his *Book of Nightmares* during a single shift.
My supervisor, uneasy with cardiac monitors,
asked me to take my break within shout's reach,
so I crawled through the window

onto the slant roof, settled just beyond the sill
where I began reading that book-length poem
by flashlight, as the Cumberlands
floated in moonlight. A nighthawk
hunted beneath me, and the terror that underlies

everything unfolded in those pages (*Lieutenant.*
This corpse will not stop burning!)
But dread was balanced by abundant
tenderness. An unusually quiet shift,
so I finished the book in short gifts of time,

and the poem's wildness helped keep me awake.
6am checks and the unit filled with light
as I woke the patients, moving with my stethoscope
through so many shades of gold and flame,
those men and women in their checked gowns

becoming part of that vision.
I knew now what I wanted to do
but of course had no idea how to do it. How does
one begin to learn to extend the almost
perfect off-rhyme of tenderness and terror?

Banish Misfortune

Is everything gone? Most everything. Then why
hurry home? Our friend is in Vermont
when she gets the call

and since there's nothing now to save, she goes
as planned to the contradance. Puts off
until next day her return to Portsmouth.

I try to imagine that. Fire guts her home
so she gives herself
to the grace of movement.

A dance partner. Assigned steps that lead
through flames. One outstretched
hand then the next.

Most things destroyed, so how can it still be possible
to be this light on her feet? She recalls
the swallow-like girls who swooped

through the house after her aunt's funeral,
playing under the table, then back in motion,
almost flying. Aunt Beatrice,

who once told her that ten years after
Uncle Derek's death, she still
reached out for him most mornings,

then got up and made her own coffee.
After the funeral, she spent the night
in her aunt's home

and saw the fox. A regular visitor. 'The fox
from the far field.' One constant
in the time of flux, a wild red flash,

though utterly unhurried, and now
she faces her partner, follows the sequence
of hands and smiles

and tries to keep moving through *Bring Me Flowers,*
The Bare Necessities,
then *Banish Misfortune.*

Her drive back to the charred
apartment awaits, her stepping through loss.
She wants these dances first, needs

to take the hand of whoever appears, *you, now,*
smiling as she casts off, fiddle and accordion
keeping things progressing.

Draws another deep breath. Does her best to take flight
like those young girls. Oh to be the age
of those swallows again.

To not yet know what disaster can bring.

Meat Loaf in the Wilds of Ireland

Once, he'd been the Texas kid who morphed
into a thunderstorm. The *Bat Out of Hell*. One wild
unsustainable flight, but then ticket sales plunged
so Meat Loaf toured the Irish midlands,
where even his credit card was rejected.

The inquisition at the ATM:
after three security questions he couldn't answer,
the Hole in the Wall told him he needed
to *call an identity specialist.*
Jeers and projectiles the night before.

The sound check delayed since the generator
hadn't arrived yet to transform the barn
into a venue. Gazing through the massive
open door into the middle of nowhere
as farmland began to blur. Who'd turn up

for a show out here? Later, describing this,
was he just ragging us when he claimed
the dark night of Meat Loaf's soul was finally lifted
by *Paradise by the Dashboard Light*?
He swore that mid-song something changed.

Five or six thousand danced in the illuminated fields
beyond him, and he felt his ragged voice
become again a force. *On stage, at least, I'd become*
a demigod, and music was once more a means
to get out of one's small life into something larger.

Hard to imagine Meat Loaf's rock-opera of a life
as small: there was that nightmare day in Dallas
when a blood-stained Jackie Kennedy was hurried
into hospital and he felt the very fabric of things
change; there was his drunken father

who tried to stab him; glimpses of the upliftingly
raunchy duets; the *Rocky Horror Picture Show*;
and all those sold-out concert halls.
But the moonlit farm in Ireland,
wherever it was they'd had him play, was anything

ever better? The beginning of the comeback
which made everything that followed possible.
And no, not a demigod, he'd become
Dionysus, and everyone danced.
For one night, at least, everyone was happy.

Estuary

Returning after decades to the same Connemara beach
we once camped above with children

I walk the length of the strand each day
turning back at the estuary

until one March morning I tuck car keys and socks
into shoes then wade into the moving water

testing if it's possible to cross. Knee deep
I study the mountains from the mouth of the river

then push on to a place of isolated inlets and dunes,
and it's like stepping out onto the sands

after my life has ended – the world goes on
as a wild, bare tassel work of rocky bluffs and coves.

A jolt of wind – rain is on the horizon –
and then a curlew calls.

When have I last heard that sound? Its liquid cry.
Clear, underwater song from one world or the other.

Pause

Seen as we returned from our neighbour's wake:
first foxgloves of the year, first sea pinks. But what things
are we seeing for the last time? We're still new

to this townland, so we never met Therese, but needed
to pay our respects. Who was this woman
who, well into her eighties, immersed herself each day

in the North Atlantic? Once home, we make a moment
for ourselves, bring gin and tonics to the garden chairs.
And see the line of rain blotting out Inishturk: five minutes

and we'll have to move inside. But what a gift
these five minutes are! Late May, winter coats
pulled tight. For these few weeks our field is radiant

with ragged robin and buttercups. Beyond it, gannets dive
into the riled waters of a transfigured world.
Because the rain cloud is now approaching

the Carrickabullog Rocks, we guess there is
what, two minutes more, so we try to take everything in
fully: the song thrush's variations,

the burst of sunlight riding just before the squall,
the yellow ambulance that heads slowly
down to the beach, no hurry, perhaps on break.

All this with a taste of lime. The first fine drops
arrive and we linger, travellers
at the border between one moment and the next.

Reading the News – Keeping Informed

in memory of Stephen Minot

There will be no internet, the retreat house director told us, smiling. *No phone reception. You'll concentrate on your work during the day, you'll put what's most urgent for you into it, then sleep deeply with vivid dreams.*

Maybe that's what it should have been like, maybe that's sort of what did happen (some of the dreams were wild), but it was our first time in the south of France, and back in the States my mother was ill. We'd seen her a few weeks earlier, but that first night in the 12th century villa, I woke and thought, isn't it just like Death to say, *You assumed you'd be there for the last breath, but you left the room to take that call ...*

All the rooms were named for muses. Ours was Thalia, after the muse of comedy, though our suite opened onto Melpomene, tragedy, the room I'd agreed to work in.

No, that's not where this is going. My mother lived another three years, and I wasn't wrong not to fly to her bedside, though every day I thought we should: how could I concentrate on writing if Mother might be dying?

*

Once, I worked with abused children. Few of those kids had nightmares as bad as the ones I had when I was five.

Mother was exhausted, coming each night to let me know everything was alright, but finally she took the advice of our family doctor, *If he's screaming, tell him you'll come three times, and after that, if he calls again, tell him you'll come, but you'll spank.*

It was worth it to me. The witch stepped from my closet, I shouted, and on her fourth visit Mom would spank me as lightly as she could and still have it count.

*

I am writing this in the middle of the night at home in Ireland, and though I tried not to check on the latest news from Ukraine, wanting to stick to my rules about not surfing the internet until morning, Russia is shelling the largest nuclear power plant in Europe, flames are rising, and who knows what will come next?

*

Mornings, I tried to write, then left the mountain after lunch for the internet café. No news at first, but on the third day my brother, the doctor, told me don't come yet, but do check in on Mom every day, just in case. Evenings, drinks on the terrace, and the owls calling out across the deep rift that makes a valley. What else is a valley but a fissure in the way things once were?

Then the effort of sleeping deeply in an antique bed that's too short to extend my legs.

Pay attention to what wakes me. What's most urgent in me might be what punctures the dream of writing in France.

*

The *Paris Review's* online newsletter has just reprinted something by my mother's brother, Stephen Minot, originally published in 1977. My uncle's piece is labelled "Prose" and begins in first person, so for some reason I think it is memoir. It's called *Reading the News—Keeping Informed,* and it's not until he writes about his daughter, and her overachieving friend who kills herself at fifteen, that I realize this must be fiction. Stephen never had a daughter.

*

Some books arrive exactly at the wrong time. *Digital Minimalism,* by Cal Newport, proposes a 30-day *digital declutter,* during which I can take a break from the constant bombardment of technology and find instead the deep connections. I know I need this book to bolster my "rules" about the internet. Just not now.

As Russia invades Ukraine, I'm not ready to cut back on reading the *New York Times* and the *Guardian*. History is in a tailspin and I don't want to turn away, I'm almost scared to sleep.

I know, breaking news is rarely as accurate as when journalists have a chance to process it, but in today's *Irish Times* Fintan O'Toole quotes Lenin: *There are decades when nothing happens, and there are weeks when decades happen*. This past week shudders under decades of news.

*

Tornados threatened as we flew to Indiana for Mom's surgery. That was two months before we left for France. My brother came too, and when the radio told him to seek shelter in a ditch he thought, *You're kidding, in this hail?* and chanced the storm in his parked car.

*

Stick to the rules. Or give up sleep. At what point will I, like the characters in Stephen's story, need a drink to find my way out of the news and back to a dream?

Cal Newport: *Humans are not wired to be constantly wired.* I need to come back to this book. Or learn from it even now.

*

When I was a boy and had surgery, Mom said, *There are two types of people, those who want someone to be with them when they're in pain and those who prefer to suffer in silence and not worry others. What sort of boy are you?* (It was clear she preferred the silent ones).

So after her surgery, how strange to hear her cry out, *Oh Mommy! Ouch*!

*

The speaker in Stephen's story makes up maddening games to get to sleep. Sleep as an act of the imagination, when this world loses its hold and we piece together a new realm, out of fragments.

*

On our first morning at the Inn of the Muses, two ripe plums appeared at our doorstep. Same thing next day, but no one knew who was leaving these gifts.

On the third morning, at the top of the village, we solved the mystery: from a loaded branch that extended over the narrow street, a plum dropped, bounced twice, rolled downhill, caromed off a wall, disappeared into the maze of lanes below. Some must have rolled all the way down our steep hills to the river. Others stopped at our door, split-open or whole.

*

Towards daybreak I read that the fire at the power plant has been extinguished, and I head to bed. But how to sleep soundly when the containment shell around a reactor might be the next target of a missile?

*

Uncle Stephen's *Paris Review* piece recounts a chance encounter with his sister's son in Stockholm—has he made up an alternate life for me? If I visited Scandinavia briefly during the Vietnam war, this guy is stuck there now, and hates the winters.

*

The mayor invited everyone for aperitifs after Mass (there are so few practicing Catholics in his village that the church only opened once a month, and after that day's service, why not hold a fête?) We drank and I hummed along to *La Marseillaise,* then *L'Internationale.* When Annie and I returned to Thalia, there were quick little lizards on the windowsills and we made love, and when have we ever been happier?

Then we drove into the city. Checked for news on Mother. No one's written for days.

*

Trying to fall asleep, I picture the narrator's nephew from my uncle's story as he would be today. Same age as me, white hair and round glasses, and let's say he's made a life for himself in Sweden.

The first customer in a café in Södermalm, he's staring at his newspaper, closing his eyes, trying to understand how troops could fire at nuclear reactors. He's been fluent in Swedish for almost half a century, but when he opens his eyes he can't understand a word.

This train of thought is not going to help me sleep. I watch the nephew pay for his coffee then walk block after block toward the bridge to the Old Town, following a route I once took. All along the street, Ukrainian flags wave from the beginning of a dream.

*

Had I managed to fall asleep before the sound of flags flapping woke me?

Quick check of the news.

The internet is still on in much of Ukraine, though Russia is working to create silence. On a

former student's blog, I read how his friend refuses
to leave Kherson, saying her cat is a better
early-warning system than the air-raid sirens:
before anyone else hears anything, the cat is at the
window, hissing.

The Hares of Lettergesh West

for Eamon Grennan

Annie, half sleeping, asks as I climb back in bed,
Have you been up long? and I don't know how
to answer – it feels like eons. Not wanting

to wake her further, I don't mention the four hares
I saw when I went out to look at stars.
Except for the swivelling of their long ears

they were motionless, as if enchanted
by the dawn chorus, and we formed
such a strange tableau: the otherworldly

hares and me, stepped out of time, and the impossible
blackbird. At last the four philosophers
loped off out of sight to their lives as hares,

and I was once more that foolish thing,
a white-haired man in pajamas. If only
they'd looked back. If only they'd let me know I'm real.

Aircoach into Dublin

Gusts struck so hard the double-decker bus shook,
and I pictured the East Anglia coach that last week

blew over – the news repeatedly showed it lift
in the air then slam on its side. Once is not enough

for such an image. I was grateful our driver
slowed as if he'd seen the same footage.

Then a long tunnel and several sheltered minutes
until we emerged to an even stronger wind.

Is it best to have your seat belt on or off
if your bus flips over? We shuddered our way

into a canyon of red brick buildings, back it seemed
to the ordinary, which was when the apparition

appeared in an open window; a young woman,
pale skin, dark hair, dressed mostly in black,

smoking as she stared up at gulls
that shot across her sliver of bleak sky. We tilted

abruptly towards her and she turned her gaze,
her free hand reaching out as if to stop us

from overturning, and what I take with me
from that journey into the city is the way, when the bus

steadied, her raised hand turned into a wave,
half amused, half terrified, before we sailed on.

LUNCHTIME CONCERT IN GALWAY: OP. 18, NO. 2

Even by Irish time, he's late. The second violinist
keeps checking her watch, the guest violist
seems to have climbed down into a Zen hole,
the first violinist makes arpeggios sound like

shimmering running-in-place, but the cellist
is elsewhere, his place held by an empty chair.
Finally he arrives, quickly tunes,
and the musicians lean forward, let themselves go,

dive into the first movement's sparkle
as if it's the easiest thing –
which, as the cellist tells us afterwards, it was.
After leaving the other driver

at the scene of the fender bender
to explain to the Gardaí –
after posting a friend outside the concert hall
to receive any official phone call

and convince them that the cellist
is inside playing Beethoven,
see, you can hear him in there, listen –
after the worry and all those hours of sleepless joy

during which his wife gave birth to their first child,
a daughter, Klara – what could be easier
than inhabiting the sunny world
of this early quartet, nothing discordant here,

no letter to the world of a crisis of the soul,
just a thanksgiving, a salutation.
The miracle of Beethoven, as if nothing were easier.
This is for Klara. This is for Andreea.

February Rain

After reading George Saunders, Swimming in a Pond in the Rain

Here in Renvyle, someone's always aware of you,
so this morning, entering the waves

in February weather, I imagined a neighbour
turning to his wife and saying, *What is Ted*
thinking, swimming alone in the rain?

What I was thinking about was Paddy Fitzpatrick,
the only person who knew the name

of the cove where I've swum almost every day
since Father's death ten years ago: Cuanín na Céibhe.
Paddy's gone now, carried last November

from wake house to grave in a coffin
shaped like a boat. *Is mór an trua:* It's a great pity.

I swam out a short way and recalled the scene
in Chekhov's 'Gooseberries' in which Ivan Ivanovich
swims in the rain with two friends, then floats

on his back as drops fall on his face and realises
he's absurdly happy. But it's this same Ivan Ivanovich

who later in the story rails against those whose happiness
is only possible if they ignore the suffering of others.
If I could speak now to the neighbours I imagined

were watching me I'd say, *What a mess*
of contradictions we all are, yourselves of course

excepted! But I'd also love to tell them
how Chekhov, as a young writer, went to visit Tolstoy,
and how anxious he was about meeting

the genius, the prophet, the *colossus*.
The novelist was walking the beech-lined road

to the river when Chekhov arrived, and the two men
ended up splashing naked in the lilies
chatting amiably, so perhaps when Chekhov

wrote 'Gooseberries' three years later
he had his visit to Yasnaya Polyana in mind?

Surely it's best to let my neighbours think I was at the cove
by myself. Imagine if word got round I thought
I was swimming in the rain with Chekhov and Tolstoy!

ARIEL

I walked to the cove for a dawn swim
on the birthday of the Scorpio of Scorpios,

trying to fathom the gift Plath had given me,
words that stung yet felt absolutely necessary.

This was 2013, just after my father's death,
a time when words were signals or flares

and there were no more poems
except the one I was living inside. Everything

connected, and I remembered the excitement
of the special collections librarian

as she showed me the *Webster's Dictionary*
in which Plath underlined or annotated

words on almost every page as she devoured
language, and it was like gazing at the birth of stars.

Under the entry for *Ariel*, Plath underscored
one definition identifying the angel

who was *the lioness of God*.
Father, I'm still trying to figure it out,

but fifty years after Plath's death
I carried her lines on my tongue to the sea

and it all had something to do with you.
Light built behind Mayo's mountains,

ready to speak. Each *red eye*, each *cauldron*
a variation on the proto-word,

or ur-word, struck from the confluence
of consciousness and flame. Ariel:

God's lioness. Plath's favourite horse. Prospero's
sprite. Another name for Jerusalem.

Blackberries

Summer seemed over until the month's gloom cleared
and glistening blackberries lined the roadside
as if celebrating the return of the sun god.
A small breeze as I walk back from my swim,
and the berries are like those of childhood,
sweet bursts with tart sparks, and what to do

with all the real sorrows, the honest worries,
when the taste of berries at the corners of my mouth
starts me talking to myself? But I'm also talking
to the world that miraculously includes me,
I'm turning a circle in the road to take in
seascape, mountains, and windblown fields,

and suddenly the twenty-one-year-old rookie
who ruled the Game of the Week five decades ago
comes to mind. Mark "The Bird" Fidrych
paced around the mound between pitches,
smoothing the dirt with his bare hand,
then concentrated by talking to the ball, telling it

just what to do. I pick a handful of berries
to bring home to my wife, wanting to tell her how
fifty thousand fans chanted the name
of the most unlikely of stars, a kid
who'd been held back in first grade, then again
in second, and suddenly was grinning

from the cover of *The Rolling Stone.*
He partook of the supersublimity of summer itself—
that must be the word for it, if there is one, *supersublimity*.
He's gone now, but if injuries shortened his career
to one glorious year, his ebullience brought him to mind
half a century later. Joy has its afterlife.

Second Lives

Returning home with a handful of blackberries for Annie,
    I hear her shout. I hurry to her
but find she'd called to see if I'd seen the pod of dolphins

    cross the bay while I was swimming. Dolphins!
Go back to Mary Isobel Catherine Bernadette O'Brien,
    graduating from convent school and bidding farewell

to short auburn hair and thick glasses so she could become
    Dusty Springfield, the glamorous blonde
who declared, *Mary O'Brien was destined to become*

    a librarian, but she isn't going to make it.
At the end of her career, she, who had become a diva,
    may have become a dolphin.

Her ashes were scattered from a cliff near Doolin
    and a dolphin appeared,
sparkling sunlight like one of her evening gowns.

    Which is when we may have met.
Thinking we were coming to Ireland for one year,
    we'd packed up our lives

and arrived on the cliffs of Clare. Jetlagged, Annie was
    second-guessing the move on our first day –
she missed our grown children, missed her friends, missed

    her library job. Then a dolphin
entered the inlet below us so we scrambled downhill,
    and when it swam towards us

we pushed off our shoes and jumped in, clothes and all,
    rejoicing. It must have been right to move here;
but even as I write these words, I imagine

Annie's rueful laugh.
Twenty-something mostly happy years later, her poems
are still haunted by where home is,

the life here and the love of those who are far away.
As if, what is hers or anybody's life
but the pattern of piecing happiness and regret together?

Song Above the Dishes

In the kitchen, to the tune of the Beatles' 'Let It Be',
Annie's singing 'Let it go, let it go',

a variation one of us came up with two decades ago
during 'the Christmas massacre'.

In a fortnight we'd lost our jobs then found far better ones,
though that meant we had to leave Donegal.

Annie's song brings back now our farewell walk
to the abandoned train station

of Caiseal na gCorr. Dear capital of emptiness. Hub
of the bleakly beautiful. Let it go.

Wind fanned waves across pools and rivulets,
and the bogs were a labyrinth of light.

Annie scanned the wet heath, hoping for one last sight
of *our* stag: that's what he'd become

since we'd seen him so often that December, raising
his antlered head to hold us in his gaze.

Possibility made him a constant presence. I started to tally
each lie our boss told,

each bit of meanness, and Annie insisted, *Don't poison
yourself.* Let it go, let it go. The lights

of Tory Island. A broken line on the North Atlantic.
And though we didn't see it,

somewhere a stag must have lowered his head to drink
from those flooded boglands.

LENINGRAD SYMPHONY

Horizontal rain at the windows and pulsatile tinnitus
pounding in my ears as I sit in the waiting room, apart
from the other patients,

and try to read an essay on Shostakovich
(he says, *Every artist who isolates himself from the world
is doomed*).

Though he wanted to finish the *Seventh Symphony* in his
besieged city,
the State evacuated him, so the final score was spirited

back to Leningrad in a small plane over German lines,
bringing with it
the problem of finding enough living musicians to play
the massive work.

The radio offers a free trip for two to Tenerife
as I try to concentrate on the rehearsals
during the Winter of Death:

a clarinetist whose reed was frozen and whose cracked lips
couldn't produce a sound;
a cellist who arrived after burying his wife, one of the
hundred thousand who starved each month;

and a percussionist who was sent to the city's morgue,
then found to be not
dead after all. *The Leningrad Symphony*. Practiced
by an orchestra formed from fragments.

Finally, half-starved musicians performed in August 1942,
some wearing gloves
on their bone hands with holes cut for fingers.

Music broadcast through almost empty streets,
out to the enemy.
By the time Doctor Alex summons me, the tinnitus –
small scourge

in the fabric of things but one that keeps me up at night –
has, of course, disappeared. Monica sets up a 24-hour
blood pressure test

and every fifteen minutes, after the cuff inflates and I've
let it read
me, I jot down what I've been doing. The first note records

walking the White Strand during a break in the gale
on the way home.
I meet no one. And revel in that solitude. Why am I
happy

not seeing anyone? Shostakovich again: *I find it incredible*
that an artist should want to shut himself away.
Always this need to reconcile

the wish for solitude with the necessity of solidarity
with others?
The cuff tightens and knows me. Oh, give me enough time
to myself and I'll try

to connect. In the afternoon, that vast symphony.
By the window, a bowl with four narcissus bulbs, like
onion domes

on an Orthodox cathedral in a war zone. How do
you practice Shostakovich an hour after burying
your wife?

I'm getting used to the quarter-hour checks, but Annie
        looks nervous
each time the motor kicks on to tighten the cuff.

Night, now, and I sleep until 4. Then the whooshing
        sound
that mirrors the pulse at my wrist returns to trouble
        both ears.

I've been told humming can briefly banish tinnitus
        so I hum Shostakovich
until the drumming stops, then return to the essay.

Survival first, but, granted that, the imperative
        of music.
Then I give myself to the songlines and rhythms of sleep.

Bruach na Carraige Báine

in memory of Séamus Begley

A late night, long ago. A snug in a Kerry pub
and the three of us talking so earnestly
when a singer's first pure notes

made us stand and listen. Has a song
ever circled a room more sweetly, promising
love worth more than the riches of Spain,

promising a coach that could journey
past the rim of the White Rocks?
Gone now, our words. Gone is that singular

voice, whose spell lingered
once his music stopped, making the silence pulse.
Stepping out into that late night, long ago,

we carried with us an unexpected gift, a song
that could take us through glistening after-hours streets
and beyond the rim of the White Rocks.

On Listening to Ciarán Hinds Play Francis Hardy in *Faith Healer*

The way silence is honoured between words. So,
  my leaning forward, listening
to the audiobook as if what's essential is the not-said.
  And when Francis Hardy
(self-professed "mountebank", whose gift for healing
  fails nine times in ten) hesitates
before confiding to us, *// We / were // in / the / north //*
  of / Scotland, ///
we're conscious of the distance to Dublin
  where his mother was dying.
He reached her bed one hour and ten minutes too late.
  I stop the recording and, in the pause
that follows, remember Father Enda Fahy.
  Half a lifetime ago,
in that Connecticut hospital cafeteria, Enda Fahy
  warily extolled Brian Friel.
Exhausted but needing to talk, he cradled
  a plastic coffee mug
as if it were a lifebuoy and said when he'd read
  Faith Healer on the plane
it seemed to prophesise he wouldn't arrive in time.
  So many anxious delays, he said.
It may be forever before I catch up with myself.
  For two days we'd waited for him.
He'd been called home from the Alaskan missions,
  and his sister Maureen
kept us updated (*Enda has motorcycled*
  to the helicopter pad,
Enda's plane has left Arctic Village airport),
  and what Maureen had needed
me to say (a nurse should know these things)
  is whether her mother would live
until Enda arrived. Poor daughter who stayed home
  as caregiver, Maureen

who would always be The Child Who Is Not
the Priest.
And the mother? Mary Fahy? She somehow knew
the morphine to ease the pain
might also stop her breathing. When I asked
if she'd like Last Rites
from the local priest, she said, *Out of the question.*
Enda will anoint me.
And he did. I wasn't in the room as witness,
but later as I ate supper
I talked with Enda, who said that staring down
at the endless Western darkness
(only the rare constellations of a village or town)
he'd taken consolation
from the Inuit elder who'd told him
the best place to die
was where you were born. Mary Fahy received
Communion from his hand
in her native Putnam, then closed her eyes. And waited.
Hours passed. She kept waiting,
praying for a Good Death. Before I left
she whispered to me,
I am so ready, but it's harder to die
than you'd ever guess.
Lifetimes spark in the shortest gap between words,
but what our lives amount to
is up for grabs. I press play and listen to Francis Hardy
talk with his father
after the chasm of twenty years. True,
no one in *Faith Healer* agrees
with his version of the story, but in Francis's telling,
his father didn't recognise him.
Shook hands like an acquaintance. Few words,
after all his travels ...

She looks nice, // he said. // Yes / I said. She looks //
great.
Hit pause again. Wait as if the silence might speak
to me once more. When did my life
become so fragmented? Loved ones always
a flight away.
I've watched a plane's shadow fly beneath us
in Ireland for the first mile or so
on the way to the States and my mother's bedside.
I've rushed through air
for a few last words with my father.
Hit play. Follow
Hardy and his companions for a different sort
of homecoming in Donegal.
Ballybeg. All our stories folded into monologues
of everlasting.
Spread across so many miles, our love.
So deeply flawed, our faith.

The Guest House

Knee pain, hip, backache, shoulder.
Just getting to this guest house took its toll.

Then the first night, I dreamt
that an elderly couple sought my help,

complaining they were riddled
with bullet holes. If the man seemed worse off,

the woman was suffering, too.
But when I examined them,

they had no wounds – *stress, that's all,*
I told them. *You're fine!* The old man

nodded. *Yes, stress, for sure,*
but you've just looked at our bodies.

The bullets left holes in our minds.
Hell, if we have them, holes in our souls!

Celebrations of an Introvert

Sixtieth birthday, in Montepulciano.
Only Annie and me in the living room restaurant
so the cook sends her daughter home,
waits on us herself. After the young granddaughter
leaves with her mother, the television plays
quietly in the side room. Some comedy
in Italian whose low voices move me
for reasons I can't explain.

That afternoon, Annie left me alone for fifteen minutes
in Monterchi's one-painting museum. Off-season,
so no one else in the room but the *Madonna del Parto.*
My mother died the year before, and my eyes
kept watering so I could barely see the painting.
Two angels hold back embroidered curtains
as Mary starts to undo her dress, ready to give birth.
Half my time spent with eyes closed. I saw her

with the whole wheel of emotions. Fastenings
unhooking as the walls began to shake.
And now, before we order, complimentary bruschettas
from the cook. Few shared words – I doubt she knows
it's my birthday – but after my first taste (garlic
and basil like angels at the corners of my mouth)
her smile when I open my eyes again.
As if I'd needed darkness to taste her gift fully.

Night Bus to Kreuzberg

The father and two girls we saw at the concert
settle behind us on the cross-city bus,

speaking happily in Turkish, pointing out things
in the wash of streets below.

'Figaro! Figaro!' sing the girls, and the father
doesn't hush them.

We're in the front row, upper level of the bus,
so Berlin glides towards us

like a dream of storefronts, the glittering coins
of lights in the windows.

Mid-journey the kids grow sleepy, their voices
like variations of the grandparents

in Bishop's poem, 'The Moose', their 'dreamy
divagation'. My mind too wants to digress,

and I'm recalling last year's trip on the M-29 bus
when this quiet energy was upside down.

Turkey was playing Germany, and we'd diverged
from our route, the taped announcements

told us the next stop was Moritzplatz
or Oranienplatz, but we were well south of schedule,

none of the streets matched up, so I pictured
crowds blocking traffic –

that night, no one was getting into Turkish Kreuzberg
in the usual way – and we stared out the window,

guessing our place in the city's maze,
processing the misinformation

and intuiting when to get off and walk home.
Brief laugh from one of the girls, then silence.

Soon after, the father's nod when he catches me
turning to look. Both daughters asleep,

heads against him, his arms around them.
Imagine the 'gentle, auditory,

slow hallucination' that turns these children
into grandparents in the bus!

But then the father wakes them, they stand up to leave,
and as if it's a game they look at us and sing, 'Figaro!'

We sing back to them and they disappear into the night.
Our grandparents, long departed, rode with us

on the M-29. Spoke to us in words we didn't know.
Even sang to us, so briefly.

Other World

On the anniversary of Mother's death
my sister called from the States to tell
how goldfinches flocked to her white birch.
Gold, too, were the birch's windblown catkins
where the finches, too many to count,

kept landing. And one bird on the lawn:
had it mistaken glass for air? Still breathing,
but it sat in the grass all day, stunned, surrounded
by the otherworldly chorus of all those birds.
Decades ago, in that other world of faith,

dozens of goldfinches feasted on thistles
as Annie and I read Julian of Norwich.
In that burnished meadow, impossibly young,
we took turns, one of us listening
and watching the undulating flight of finches

while the other read about Julian's visions
during the Black Plague. Today,
my sister's description of the finches
sounded like a vision in her own back yard, a visual
music in which gold notes swooped in

to land in the staves of glowing catkins,
that swung in the breeze so the melody
kept changing. Gold notes, gold catkins,
and a seemingly doomed bird
that flew back into sunlit boughs.

'BECAUSE I COULD NOT STOP FOR DEATH –'

A tumult of birds in a thicket made me pause
just before something small and brown

blazed across the path, landing on a holly limb.
How improbable: an owl the size of a sparrow.

Having mobbed the predator away,
the other birds' clamour ceased,

and the day grew large and silent. Death,
you were not quite six inches tall.

If I reached out I might have touched you.
Or was that owl Life itself? Fierce yellow eyes

burning to continue. Which means
feasting on songbirds. It shrugged

and flew off. Northern pygmy owl.
Impossibly small. Fiery as a Dickinson couplet.

Restoration of the Sleeping Buddha

After the article on tactical nuclear weapons
kept me awake, I read Dervla Murphy's travelogue,
though it proved anything but soothing:

a ripped-out bike tyre on Afghanistan's
Shibar Pass; rescue by a bus
that promptly broke down near a precipice;

a night of lightning, hailstones,
and gale-force wind; then guns
pulled when the driver raised the fare.

But from her clifftop room next morning,
she gazed past a shining valley to the world's
tallest Buddhist statues carved into a mountain.

Closing my eyes, I neared a dream
until I wondered if those two standing Buddhas
were the ones the Taliban blew up.

Yes, they watched over those villages
1,500 years
until dynamite brought them down.

Close by, an Afghan archeologist found
the remains of a third statue.
A Sleeping Buddha.

In his seventies, the archeologist said
he'd like to use his remaining years
to restore the statue.

I shut my eyes again. Recalled Thich Nhat Hanh's
gentle answer to a girl who asked
how to fall asleep quickly:

I don't think it's good to try to sleep quickly.
The more you try, the more difficult it is.
I think, therefore I cannot sleep.

And for one marvellous sliver of a night
I stopped trying
to sleep. Bicycled instead through Afghanistan,

and found it just as Dervla described. Luminous.
The silver of sinjit trees. The honeycomb
of monks' cells worked into limestone heights.

Shepherd boys driving their flocks
beneath the giant Buddhas.
Then there was something I knew *didn't*

come from the book:
Annie and I were there, gazing silently out
at the liminal valley.

All we had to do was breathe.
The whole night world opened up
between the exhale and the inhale of a breath.

Merton, Laughing

Dream fragment in which Thomas Merton
stops his Jeep at the border, where a customs official
who looks like my sister opens his suitcase
and, finding a spare monastic robe, tries it on.
When she twirls around, arms raised above her head
as if fully inhabiting the latest flamenco fashion,
Merton cries out with mirth.

My turn to cross the border next, but no one
is there. An ornate archway
leads to courtyard after blossoming courtyard.
All night, gates open, gates close. I pass through
countless gardens, but never find such joy again.
The merriment in the Trappist's face.
The moment when the official lost herself in dance.

On the Jazz Meditations of Thomas Merton

Taking a break during my nephew's rehearsal dinner,
I stepped out
onto moonlit Muhammad Ali Boulevard
where a historical plaque
marked the spot where a Trappist monk once had a vision.

In Louisville
to do errands for his abbey, Thomas Merton fell in love
with strangers hurrying past.
Cloistered so long, it felt *like waking from a dream*
of separateness.

Turning about in a circle, Merton laughed, finding
he belonged to others.
But he knew at least, *There was no way*
of telling people
they were all walking around shining like the sun.

That night I found
an archived radio programme called *Thomas Merton,*
Jazz Monk, featuring experimental
meditations he made in his hermitage. A decade
after his vision, race riots

rocked Louisville, and an hour north of the monastery
protestors were being tear-gassed.
Merton stayed up late, making a tape from a recording
of *Hoochie Cooche Man.*
As Jimmy Smith unleashed long licks on his Hammond B-3,

one hand laying down the bass
while the other followed solos long into the night,
Merton added improvised comments.
Jimmy, you're right, he called out, *Here I sit*
and the wheels

are turning. I'm listening to you, man.
    Always the need to wake
from our dream of separateness. Solitude and solidarity,
    twinned in the Kentucky knobs.
The moon's shining and the wheels are turning! Yes!

Quartet for the End of Time

Preface

Stalag VIII A, Görlitz, 1942

Let's away to prison, we two alone will sing like birds. The concert for the end times, begun before his birth. The poems his mother wrote for him when he was in her womb. The sounds of his father translating Shakespeare into French.

And the way the camp's privations forced him to formulate his credo: *I am convinced that joy exists, convinced that the invisible exists more than the visible, and that joy is beyond sorrow, and beauty is beyond horror.*

I

Saint-Julien-du-Sault, 1942/1962

The doctor was summoned by two railway switchmen
who found the escaped prisoner unconscious by the tracks,
a battered clarinet sheltered under his arm. He promised

he would bring the man to the authorities after treating
the wounds and concussion, but instead the doctor
risked his life and hid the musician from the Germans,

and though the war continued, the doctor remembered,
decades later, that month as one of laughter and stories.
And the night before he left, the fugitive Henri Akoka

played the strangest solo, some of it just on the edge
of hearing. He apologised for the swollen hand that made
fingering difficult and said he shouldn't be playing

the piece at all, it was one of eight movements,
but since a fellow prisoner wrote it for him, it was partly
his, and he had nothing else to thank the doctor.

Since the music was dedicated by its composer
to the Angel of the Apocalypse who announced,
And there shall be no more time, Akoka had the doctor

remove the clock from the drawing room so its regularity
wouldn't interfere with the unconventional rhythms.
In honour of that solo concert, the clock remained

banished to the kitchen. Such a strange piece, begun
at night near a battlefield, finished in prison, but capable
of filling the room with terrifying praise, so that briefly

the house became foreign as the moon as the music
slowed down so much that each cup, each lamp and chair
seemed inexplicably itself, a pilgrim nearing its goal.

There was nothing the doctor could lay his hand
on with certainty. Twenty years, so he has stopped hoping
for a return visit. What an odd thank-you gift and farewell.

In his work, many times the doctor has sat up late
with life and death, but only once did a grateful patient
offer in return a private glimpse of the Apocalypse.

II

Messiaen volunteered for
night duty

so he could listen
for his blackbird and

transcribe
each day's first notes

and the variations
that followed

the variations that made
music over Verdun

was that even possible
music one could live inside

III

Aix-en-Provence, 1942/Görlitz, 1941

After a third nightmare, Stéphane followed
his hands downstairs for cognac then paused
at the open window to listen as some bird held forth,

and he was right on the edge of understanding
as he recalled the stretcher and being carried
to the barracks hall for a concert, an experience

so strange he almost doubted it happened.
He'd been delirious his first days as a prisoner-of-war
in Görlitz, but that eerie spell of almost madness

was over by the time of the concert; he had been lucid.
Even so, the quartet that unfolded on the makeshift stage
seemed dreamlike. Those odd clothes the musicians wore:

patched uniforms of Czech soldiers and wooden clogs.
And the music wasn't Bach or Brahms
or anything he knew what to do with but something

written in camp by one of the prisoners,
a man in thick glasses who introduced the concert
by saying he'd been inspired by a blackbird

near a battlefield at 3am, or else by the Angel
of the Apocalypse. Stéphane paused, savouring
the last drops of cognac and their scent, recalling

a clarinet that seemed to transcend terror and find
some sort of consolation. He didn't believe in miracles,
but if they existed, that's what it must feel like

to be inside one, notes stretching out forever
and a sort of trembling all around him
that he couldn't be sure was real. He remembered

wondering during the concert how, after such music,
anyone could go back to the normal world. Was
there still such a thing as normal? That would be

the miracle, the ordinary. It turned out, of course,
that he couldn't return to his teaching duties. What,
really, could he have offered his students

when something at his core was filled with horror?
Still, a blackbird called a new day into being
and a valley full of birds answered.

He doubted the nightmares would stop
even if the war ended, but he promised himself
he would get up tomorrow night and at least listen.

IV

As if knitting by dawn's window was a way
of making something

out of the cut-short the unknown
the fragmented

a way of responding to the
listening

a way of staying in communication
in communion

a way

V

Aix-en-Provence, 1944

Away. She wonders if it was Penelope, not Homer,
who wove together Odysseus's story, creating a narrative
from what little was told and all that was left unsaid,

some sort of myth to make sense of a reluctant
soldier's life. She doesn't know how to weave,
though she can knit; she can cast on the foundation

of beginnings, stitch upon stitch, dawn upon dawn.
It doesn't banish sorrow, but it feels somehow necessary
to continue this broken conversation.

She never did learn what Stéphane's time was like
in the German prison camp – for him to have spoken
of those things would have been to remember.

But one night – maybe two years ago – she joined him
by the window where he liked to sit, and found him
half-moving his mouth with eyes closed. She asked

if she was disturbing his prayers, and Stéphane frowned,
said he was done with prayer, he was just
listening. When the blackbird stopped singing, he shook

as he told her about a concert he'd once heard in prison.
Most nights after that she'd make coffee
and sit near him, knitting, and if he didn't share

anything else about the war, at least they made
a shared space of that silence.
Almost a year now since his death. Odd that it wasn't war

that killed him but influenza she might have brought
home from selling her wares in the market.
Sometimes rising so early is simply exhausting,

but now that he's gone, she can say to the empty seat: *I like*
the prayer of first coffee, and the prayer of opening the window.
I like the prayer of waiting, and the prayer of needles

meeting and clicking. Song upon song upon song:
soon, she thinks, this morning's bird will speak,
and before that it was music Stéphane heard

in a barracks hall, and before that a bird some composer
listened to in an army camp before the sun. As if
the beauty we can hear and see is always preceded

by another one that joins us. There, now, this day's
first note, sounding like a slightly despondent question.
Impossible to explain to parents or friends

why she should keep getting up early to greet the day.
He couldn't explain it, and she can't either,
but it's important to be here each night at the window,

listening. The soft sound of needles
as she knits it all in, beauty and sorrow, beginning with
the one sung word from which everything else follows.

VI

Because Olivier-Eugène-Prosper-Charles Messiaen
could no more receive his former guard

or meet or mistake him
since Time never passes not really not fully

until it does
but this was not the true fullness of Time

very near but not yet forever

VII

Paris, 1991

Grateful to have his mind intact this long – to be able
to create works of praise in his eighties –
though surgery pulls at the threads of time, anesthesia

alters the fit of things. Surgery and time: he can play
with the way his days are revised, express musically
how this morning, troubled that he'd recently declined

an invitation to the premiere of his quartet –
after all that work, a shame not to be there – then realised
that the premiere was fifty years ago, this must be

the great, great, great, great granddaughter
of that first concert. A slight confusion then,
but temporary, his memory is still there, just needing

orchestration, so he's left with the awareness
of all he's done, and what's been left undone. He woke
remembering picking fiery flowers in a meadow

in the afterlife for his dead wife –
petals like asphodels, but flaming red, and rising
in a healing swirl – it was important that he approach her

with gifts as she had something important to tell him.
Surgery it seems can throw the circadian clock
into some new rhythm, the fabric of the everyday

begins to unravel, and one can wake as if in the claws
of a time change. He had declined
the fiftieth-anniversary concert of the quartet

which was to be performed in the prison camp
where it was born: too many nightmares there,
and, of course, the problem of these blessed vertebrae.

But that invitation allowed the guard
he'd nearly forgotten to enter from stage left –
Karl-Albert Brüll, who gave him paper and pencils,

sometimes extra bread, and a quiet place to work
in the middle of the Stalag. His back, his back, his back
is killing him, and he pleads for pain relievers.

After the premiere, Brüll forged papers for his release,
making them look legal with a seal carved from a turnip –
no, a potato! What is left for him to do

with Time? Decades had passed when Brüll tried
to visit him in Paris, but that was 1968, the year his work
was disrupted, the year President de Gaulle

briefly fled the country as students occupied concert halls
and theatres, and workers joined them to barricade
Latin Quarter streets. What could he do? He told

the concierge he couldn't see Brüll. Shouldn't it
have been possible, in all that upheaval,
for the former prisoner to find a way to speak

with his former guard? The graffiti near the church
where he played organ comes back: *Be realistic,
ask the impossible.* Years too late, he tried

to contact him, but Brüll had died in an accident. Once,
there was a chance for reconciliation, but any child
of the street knows chances are like sparrows.

Time, he thought, is one of the strangest creatures
of God, but one day, at the world's end, Time itself
will be reunited with Eternity.

When Paris is turned upside down again,
as it must be, if he is to waken fully, he will need
those fire flowers to approach his former guard.

He is conscious of age, but there are many conversations
to finish: with Claire, so long dead now,
with the German, Brüll, with this new composition

that has something to do with the endlessness
of the moment. And just how long
does it take to bring those pills?

VIII

Because from the beginning from the
birthplace from the beacon

it was all fullness it was
ripeness it was all we could have

hoped for
and though we were imprisoned

we could still be *God's spies*
oh it should have been simple

when thou dost ask me
blessing I'll kneel down

and ask of thee forgiveness
it should have been so easy –

No no no no no of course not
there is finally only the mercy

Lullaby Before Leaving Again

How unlikely. Three perfect weeks of weather
in Connemara. Propped in bed, photographing
the wall mirror where the glass has pulsed
each evening with reflections of sky and sea,

so I wish I could paint it (Bonnard, I think,
or Matisse – the mirror, the window,
the wash of waves) and the photograph
or painting I've been inside sunset after sunset

has something to do with the bright
red and purple flare of endlessness
framed in the window, reframed in the mirror,
which is when Annie enters the room,

and she and her handsewn blue kimono
are doubled in the glass. The high pressure system,
usually stalled above the Azores,
is lingering over us as if we could wander forever

in these no-longer-recognisable rooms
through light that seems Mediterranean.
Annie, in her kimono, pauses before the mirror
that is in and out of the dream. Endlessness,

balanced with the news we'll have to leave
this place. Isn't that where we started?
We don't know the least of it.
Still, there is this moment:

Matisse. Bonnard. The open window.
The benedictions of water and shore.
And a kimono the colour of Clare
and Achill and Inishturk, just as the sun sets.

Acknowledgements

Thanks to the editors of the following journals in which these poems first appeared:
Atticus Review: Lullaby before Leaving
The Cormorant: The Quarrel
Crannóg: Blackberries
Cyphers: Still Listening for the Coyle Brothers, Lunchtime Concert in Galway
Dunes Review: Leningrad Symphony
Honest Ulsterman: Aircoach into Dublin
HOWL: New Irish Writing: One Moment
The Irish Times: The Hares of Lettergesh West
On the Seawall: Souvenir of the Gone World
Poetry Ireland Review: Meat Loaf in the Wilds of Ireland
Skylight 47: February Rain
Sojourners: Merton, Laughing

Quotations from Galway Kinnell in 'On Three Poems by Galway Kinnell' are used by permission of The Literary Estate of Galway Kinnell, LLC.

Many thanks to Betsy Sholl, Moya Roddy, Pete Mullineaux, Geraldine Mitchell, and Annie Deppe for their thoughts about these poems.

About the Author

Theodore Deppe is the author of *Beautiful Wheel*, *Liminal Blue* and *Riverlight* (Arlen House, 2014, 2016 and 2019); *Orpheus on the Red Line* (Tupelo, 2009); *Cape Clear: New and Selected Poems* (Salmon, 2002); *Children of the Air* and *The Wanderer King* (Alice James Books, 1990 and 1996).

He holds a Master of Fine Arts degree from Vermont College. A recipient of two grants from the National Endowment for the Arts and a Pushcart Prize, he has been writer-in-residence at the James Merrill House in Stonington, Connecticut, and Phillips Academy in Andover, Massachusetts.

Ted has taught creative writing in graduate programmes in the US, Ireland and England. For many years, he directed the Stonecoast in Ireland residencies, which brought graduate students from the University of Southern Maine to study in Ireland.

He worked as a registered nurse for twenty years while teaching poetry and fiction classes. Since 2000, he and his wife, poet Annie Deppe, have, for the most part, made their home on the west coast of Ireland. They presently live in Connemara. He is a dual citizen of the US and Ireland.